CAT NAV

For Tommy, a big, friendly, black-and-white cat
who sings "Karma Chameleon" in my dreams

First published in 2008 by Prion
An imprint of the Carlton Publishing Group
20 Mortimer Street
London W1T 3JW

A CIP catalogue record for this book is available from the British Library

ISBN: 978-1-85375-687-0

Editor: Martin Corteel
Project Art Editor: Katie Baxendale
Production: Oliver Jeffreys
Jacket illustration: Mike Mosedale

Printed in Dubai

CAT NAV

A MAD MOGGY'S ROAD ATLAS OF
GREAT BRITAIN & IRELAND

MIKE MOSEDALE

PRION

Introduction

Drive a blindfolded moggy several miles from his home and leave him without a map, compass or GPS system and lo and behold he'll turn up on the doorstep within a day or two: unless your neighbour also feeds him in which case it'll be whoever happens to be wielding the tin opener.

It's a complete waste of a remarkable ability. If you could only harness moggy direction finding to the family motor it would be possible to dispense with the worthless piece of dysfunctional kit that you were persuaded to have installed at considerable cost. True, your map reading skills were questionable and in the past your refusal to demean yourself by asking a complete stranger for help, infuriated your better half, but who needs a garish multicoloured plastic screen stuck on your tasteful dashboard, and who needs a pseudo mid Atlantic voice telling you that 'You have arrived'.

Cats should be made to work for their living. With the proper training and incentives we could get these pampered pets up and running. Imagine a world free of the curse of in-car satellite navigation. Think of the environmental benefits of dispensing in the manufacture and eventual disposal of these cursed instruments.

Their interpretation of place names might be difficult for us to understand and their knowledge of the highway code a definite miss, but one things for certain… a cat will always get you home.

CAT NAV GOES DOWN YOUR WAY

ENGLAND & WALES

'RANDY OLD BUGGERS!'

'ONLY HAPPENS TO ME WHEN I GET TENSE.'

'MINE'S MORE OF AN ORNAMENTAL SHRUB!'

'I FEEL A LITTLE STIFF MYSELF.'

'BLOCKED PUB TOILETS...DON'T YA JUST LOVE 'EM.'

'I'M NOT MUCH OF A ONE FOR CHEESE, MYSELF.'

'COULD'VE BUGGERED 1,000 YEARS OF HISTORY.'

'NEVER PAYS TO ARGUE WITH THEM...HEIL!'

'JUST OPEN THE BASTARD TIN YOUR REVERENCE!'

'BUY ONE, GET ONE FREE!'

'AND NOW HE'S UP AGAIN.'

'SOMETHING FOR THE WEEKEND, SIR?'

I WOULDN'T FANCY SUPPING WITH HIM!'

'RESPECT YOUR ELDERS, I SAY!'

'NO, BUT IF YOU INSIST.'

'GET OVER IT, BIG MAN!'

'DIG IT.'

'A REALLY GRIM DISCOVERY!'

'SOME TOGA PARTY THAT'LL BE!'

'NO HOPE, MATE!'

'IT'S HOPE I FEEL SORRY FOR!'

'STAY AWAY FROM THE LIGHT...'

'... EIGHT, NINE, TEN. COMING READY OR NOT!'

'HAVE I GOT KNEES FOR YOU.'

'A HARMLESS ENOUGH PASTIME!'

'SEEMS A SHAME TO WAKE HIM.'

'I MAY HAVE SEEN HIM IN A MOVIE...OR TWO!'

'STOP THE CAR! I'M BURSTING...'

'IF ALL ELSE FAILS, READ THE INSTRUCTIONS.'

'IT'S CERTAINLY NOT NICE!'

'A PAINFUL BUT ENTERTAINING TRADITION.'

'PARTY ON, DADDY-O!'

'THERE'S ALWAYS ONE.'

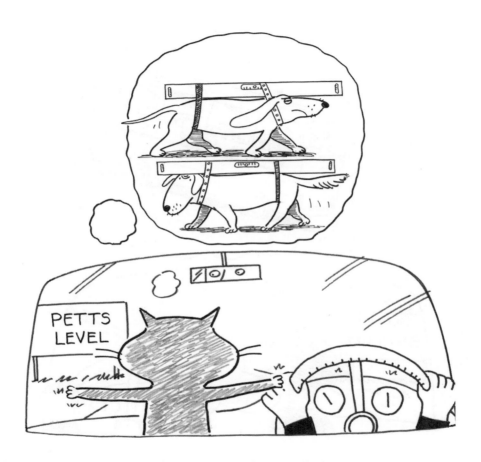

'CAN'T SEE WHAT PURPOSE IT SERVES.'

'NOT AN AREA OF OUTSTANDING NATURAL BEAUTY!'

'AH! THE DISTINCTIVE SMELL OF A DECEASED CLERGYMAN!'

'NO RHYME, NO REASON.'

'MAKES ME BLOODY ANGRY TOO!'

'I RECOMMEND YOU AVOID TRAP 2!'

'OF DESPOND, I'M TOLD.'

'WILL IT COME OUT IN THE WASH?'

'MINE'S WILTED IN THE SUN.'

'YEAH, DON'T LET HIM GO OUT!'

'FANCY BUTTOCK FLOSS, MORE LIKE.'

'DISAPPOINTING...THOUGH NOT UNEXPECTED.'

'YES I'M AFRAID SOME OF THEM ARE.'

'THERE'S NOTHING WORSE!'

'WHERE'S YOUR BROLLY?'

'YEAH GIVE IT A REST, WILL YOU!'

'COULD DO WITH A BAA OF COAL TAR SOAP.'

'IT'S CHRISTMAS KNITWEAR ALL YEAR LONG!'

'TENCH...SHUN!'

'WHAT DO YOU EXPECT WITH DENTIST'S FEES NOWADAYS!'

'I'VE A STRANGE CRAVING FOR A TATTOO.'

'AND WHAT HAVE YOU GOT? A SORE THROAT.'

'I'VE NEVER SEEN THE POINT OF IT MYSELF!'

CAT NAV TAKES THE LOW ROAD

SCOTLAND

'SAYS WHO?'

'NOW THAT'S WHAT I CALL A BUILDER'S BOTTOM!'

'IS THAT LIKE...A CAT BURGLAR?'

'BURN RUBBER BABY!'

'FULL OF STRANGE YOLK NO DOUBT!'

'I BLAME IT ON TWICE MONTHLY COLLECTIONS!'

'DON'T WORRY KEN, IT LOOKS BIGGER IN MILLIMETRES!'

'IT DOESN'T WORK FOR EVERYONE.'

'SOMEBODY OUGHT TO TELL HER.'

'ALWAYS SENDS A SHIVER DOWN MY SPINE!'

'I ONLY USE IT AS A LAST RESORT.'

'TOTALLY UNNECESSARY AND UNCALLED FOR!'

'WELL ANYTHING'S BETTER THAN A COMB OVER.'

'THINK I'LL STICK TO CHICKEN WINGS.'

CAT NAV JIGS AROUND THE EMERALD ISLE

'HE CERTAINLY TAKES NO PRISONERS!'

'SMELLS A BIT FISHY TO ME.'

'TRY NOT TO SQUEEZE IT!'

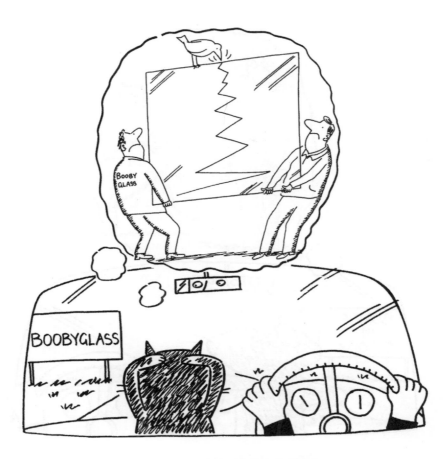

'WATCH OUT FOR LOOSE CHIPPINGS.'

'I DON'T THINK 'OSSORY' IS LOOKING TOO PLEASED!'

'LIKE A DONKEY ONLY LOUDER!'

'SHE DOESN'T LOOK TOO BAD IN HALF LIGHT!'

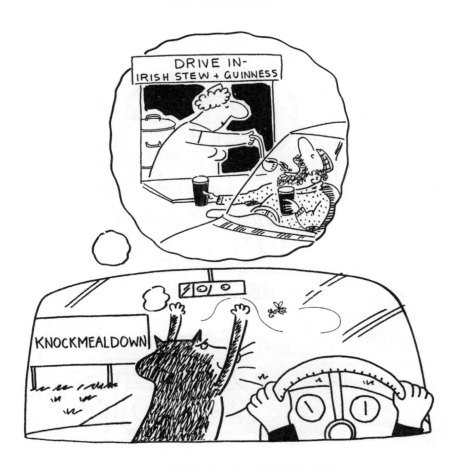

'YOU CAN'T BEAT FAST FOOD!'

'THERE WAS A YOUNG MAN FROM...'

"I'D GIVE IT TEN MINUTES, IF I WAS YOU!"

'AS THE ACTRESS SAID TO THE BISHOP.'

'WELL IF YOU CAN'T STAND THE HEAT...'

'I BLAME IT ON "FATHER TED" MYSELF!'

'WOULDN'T WANT TO SEND THE YOUNG FABIANS THERE.'

Mike Mosedale is a cartoonist and illustrator. His cartoons have appeared in many UK newspapers and magazines including: *The Times*, *The Daily Telegraph*, the *Mirror*, the *European*, the *Oldie* and the *New Statesman*.